Series consultant: Brian Williams
Author: Michael Chinery
Educational consultant: Brenda Cook

Illustrators: Craig Austin (pages 89–97)
Ian Jackson (cover and pages 11–45)
Terence Lambert (pages 47–63)
Kevin Maddison (black silhouettes)
Alan Male (pages 65–87, 107 & 110–119)
David Wright (page 106)

Designer: Caroline Johnson
Editor: Camilla Hallinan

First American edition, 1993

Copyright © 1992 by Grisewood & Dempsey Ltd./Larousse Jeunesse.
All rights reserved under International and Pan-American Copyright
Conventions. Published in the United States by Random House, Inc.,
New York. Originally published in Great Britain by Kingfisher Books, a
Grisewood & Dempsey Company, and Larousse Jeunesse in 1992.

YOUNG WORLD is a trademark of Random House, Inc.

Library of Congress Cataloging in Publication Data
Chinery, Michael.
  All kinds of animals / by Michael Chinery.
  —1st American ed.
    p. cm.—(Young world; 1)
Includes index.
  Summary: Introduces the habitat and behavior of
various animals around the world.
  1. Animals—Juvenile literature. [1. Animals.]
I. Title. II. Series: Young world (New York, N.Y.)
QL49.C533   1993
591—dc20   92–21677

ISBN 0–679–83697–7
ISBN 0–679–93697–1 (lib.bdg.)

Manufactured in Spain
1 2 3 4 5 6 7 8 9 10

YOUNG WORLD

All Kinds
of Animals

Random House 🏠 **New York**

About YOUNG WORLD

For every young child, the world is full of new discoveries, new knowledge. It is important to have information books that enable even the youngest children to enjoy making these discoveries and gathering this knowledge for themselves.

YOUNG WORLD introduces a wide range of the topics that absorb children. The books in this series are all carefully prepared by specialist authors with the help of experienced educational advisers and teachers so that information is presented simply and memorably. Each book is complete in itself, yet builds into a multi-volume set – a real encyclopedia for the vital first years at school.

Because YOUNG WORLD books are small and easy to handle, children can dip into them on their own or read them with the help of a parent or a teacher. On every eye-catching page, a great deal of thought has been put into matching the clear, readable text with beautiful illustrations. These books are designed to encourage children to find facts for themselves, opening the door to a world where discovering and learning is fun.

Brian Williams, series consultant

About this book

Wherever we are, animals of some kind or another are all around us, whether it is a fly crawling up a window pane, a spider spinning its web in the garden, or a tiger stalking its prey on a television program. If you are like me, you will want to know what they are doing, how they do it, and (always more difficult to explain) why they are doing it.

In this book I introduce all the major groups of animals, and with the help of pictures tell you wonderful facts about them. I have included a wide variety of animals from many different parts of the world, and explain how they live and why they behave as they do. As the title suggests, this book is about all kinds of animals. It is a starting point to understanding their fascinating world.

Michael Chinery, author

CONTENTS

BIRDS

REPTILES

AMPHIBIANS

FISH

OTHER ANIMALS

All kinds of

animals

🐾 What is an animal?

Animals are living things. So are plants. They both need energy for living. But they get their energy in different ways.

Plants use the sun's energy. Animals cannot do that.

Animals get their energy from the food they eat. Some eat plants, some eat other animals, and some eat plants and animals.

Humans are animals. Like tiny snails and big giraffes, we breathe and feed and grow.

✤ Animals are related

There are many different kinds of animals.
Scientists arrange them in groups.

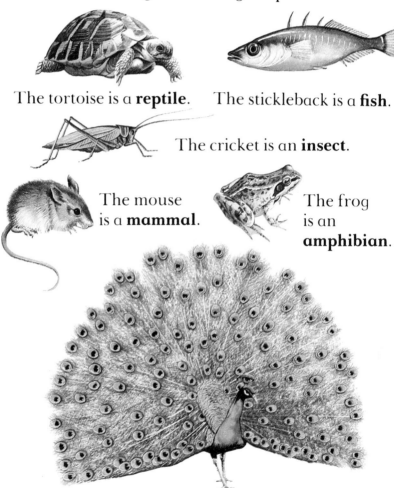

The tortoise is a **reptile**. The stickleback is a **fish**.

The cricket is an **insect**.

The mouse
is a **mammal**.

The frog
is an
amphibian.

The peacock is a **bird**.

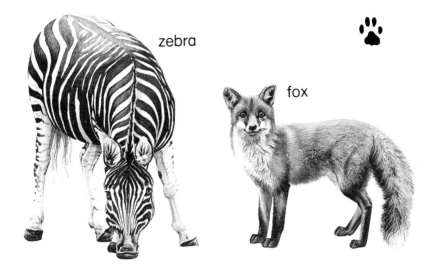

zebra

fox

All the members of a group have similar
features. The animals on this page are all
mammals. They are more closely related to
each other than to birds or reptiles or fish.

panda

brown bear

🐾 How many animals?

There are over 1 million kinds, or species, of animals. Each one is different.

Scientists divide all the species into two main groups. The animals with backbones are called vertebrates. The animals without backbones are called invertebrates.

The two main groups are divided into smaller groups. You can find out about these groups in the rest of this book.

Some species are dying out because their homes and their food supplies are destroyed when people cut down forests, drain marshes, or pollute rivers and seas.

4,000 amphibians   4,150 mammals   6,500 reptiles

VERTEBRATES

This chart shows you
how many species
there are
in each
group.

8,800 birds   21,500 fish   A million others

INVERTEBRATES

🐾 Invisible animals

Many animals are so small that you need a strong microscope to see them. Hundreds of them would fit on just one pinhead.

Many microscopic animals live in water.

The tiny paramecium might not look like an animal, but it moves and feeds, so it is an animal.

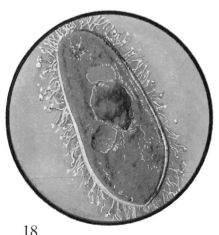

The paramecium swims through water by waving rows of tiny hairs.

It also uses the hairs to wave food into its mouth.

Mammals

🐘 What is a mammal?

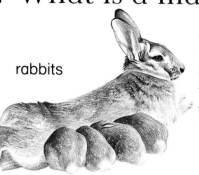

rabbits

Mammal babies feed on milk from their mother's body.

All mammals have hair on their bodies. Some have a thick furry coat to keep them warm in cold weather.

We are mammals too.

Most mammals live on land and move on four legs.

20

Some mammals hunt other animals for food. These meat-eaters are called carnivores.

Others, such as this rabbit, are herbivores — they eat only plants.

Mammals can hear and see and smell things around them.

Whiskers help this rabbit feel things as well.

Some mammals use their fingers and toes to grasp things.

🐘 Monkeys and apes

Monkeys and apes spend a lot of time in trees, so they need to be good at balancing.

Monkeys and apes can grasp things. They can pick up food, swing through trees, and...

mandrill

...hold on to their mothers when they are young and need to be carried.

baboon

Monkeys have tails. Some monkeys use their tails as well as their hands and feet to hold on to branches.

spider monkey

Apes do not have tails,
but they use both hands
and feet to swing
from trees...

gibbon

...and to hold their
young ones.

orangutan

Apes are clever.
A chimp can use
a stick to poke
termites from
their nest.

chimpanzee

🐘 Gorillas

Gorillas are the largest of the apes. They may look fierce, but in fact they are shy, gentle herbivores. They feed mainly on leaves in the forest.

Like humans, gorillas live in families. They behave like us in other ways too – they play together, stand upright, and cuddle their babies.

 Busy rodents

Beavers are rodents that use their teeth to
gnaw down small trees to dam streams and
make lakes. On the lakes, they build homes
called lodges. The beavers store twigs and
sticks in the water, to eat during the winter.

All rodents have very strong front teeth.

Squirrels grasp nuts with their front paws and crack the nuts open with their teeth.

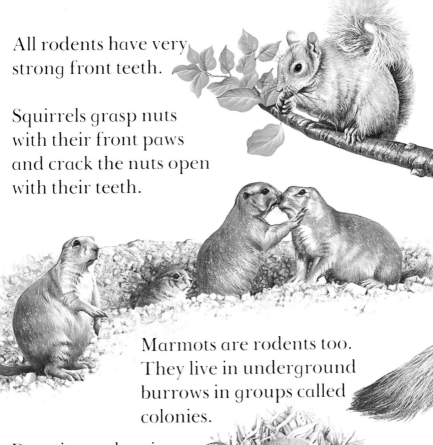

Marmots are rodents too. They live in underground burrows in groups called colonies.

Dormice curl up in cozy nests and sleep during the cold winter. For the rest of the year they sleep by day and feed at night.

27

🐘 Living in a herd

Some mammals live in large groups which we call packs or herds.

Wolves live and hunt in packs. There may be as many as 40 wolves in a single pack. Together, several wolves can chase and corner a big animal that one wolf could not catch on its own.

Herbivores, the plant-eating animals, are often safer living in a herd. If one of them sees or hears or smells danger, it warns the rest. Caribou and other deer live in herds.

🐘 Small cats, big cats

All cats are carnivores, which means they eat other animals. They use their big eyes and their excellent hearing and sense of smell to find their prey. Prey is a word for the animals being hunted.

Long tails help cats to keep their balance when they run and jump.

cheetah

cat   wild cat   lynx

Some of the big cats are very fast. A cheetah can run at 70 miles per hour.

Cats have big padded paws so they can creep up on their prey without being heard.

They have long, sharp teeth and claws to grip and kill their prey.

leopard

black panther

lions

Most cats live alone, but lions live together in groups called prides.

31

🐘 Tigers

Tigers are the biggest cats. They live in grasslands and forests. Their stripes make them difficult to see among the trees and tall grasses.

Like most cats, tigers live and hunt alone. They eat deer and wild pigs.

Tiger cubs are born blind, like the young of all cats. They do not open their eyes until they are two weeks old. At first they feed on their mother's milk.

The mother looks after her cubs for about two years, and teaches them to hunt.

🐘 Biggest on land

tusk

Elephants are the biggest
of all animals on land.
They can grow as tall as
11 feet and weigh as
much as 6½ tons.

trunk

Elephants use their long trunks to reach
food and water and carry it to their mouths.

Elephants are so strong that they can push
over trees to get at the leaves and twigs.

Biggest of all

The biggest animal of all is the blue whale, a mammal that lives in the sea. Yet it feeds only on tiny shrimp. It has no teeth, but strips of whalebone, called baleen, hang at the sides of its mouth.

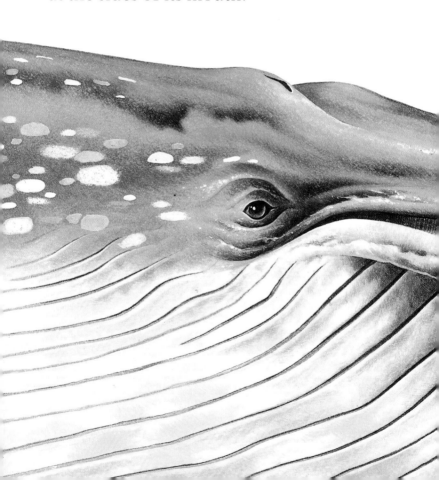

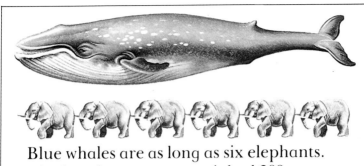

Blue whales are as long as six elephants.
The heaviest one ever weighed 209 tons.

When the whale takes a huge mouthful of water, the water escapes through the baleen, but the shrimp are trapped.

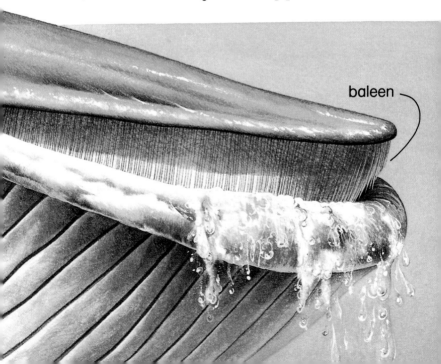

baleen

In the water

The hippopotamus spends most of the day in rivers and lakes, to keep cool. It comes out of the water at night to feed on grasses and other plants.

Seals live in the sea. With their powerful flippers they are good swimmers, and they dive down deep to catch fish. They come ashore to sunbathe and have their babies. Seals cannot walk on their flippers – instead they wriggle along the ground.

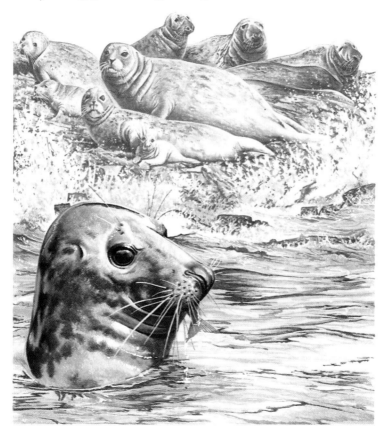

🐘 Polar bears

Polar bears live in the cold Arctic. Their thick white coats keep them warm and make them difficult to see on the ice.

They are good swimmers, and they catch fish and seals to eat.

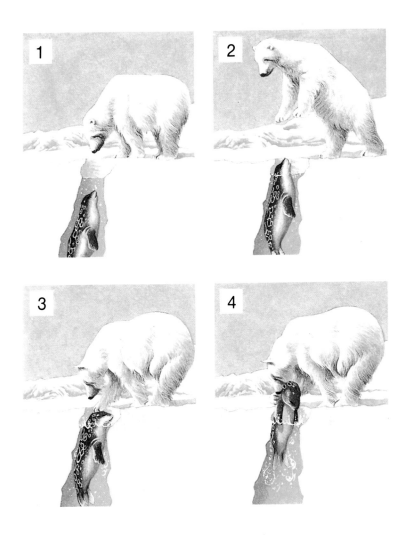

Sometimes a polar bear waits beside a hole
in the ice until a seal comes up for air.

 Pouches

Koalas belong to a group of mammals called marsupials. Although they are often called koala bears, koalas are not really bears. They eat no meat, just eucalyptus leaves.

Baby marsupials are born very small. They crawl straight into a pouch on their mother's body. They are kept safe in the pouch while they feed on their mother's milk and grow.

The baby kangaroo is called a joey.

opossums

Opossums and wombats are marsupials too.

kangaroos

wombats 43

This mammal can fly

Bats are the only mammals that can fly. Their wings are folds of skin stretched over long fingers, and they have fur on their bodies.

When a bat flies, it makes high-pitched squeaks.

The squeaks bounce off other objects all around, and the bat can hear the echoes. This is why bats do not bump into anything, even in the dark.

The echoes also bounce back from other animals, which is how bats find their food. Most bats feed on insects.

Bats sleep upside down in caves and hollow trees.

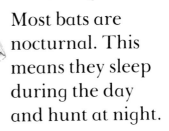

Most bats are nocturnal. This means they sleep during the day and hunt at night.

The flying fox, the largest bat of all, eats fruit. Some other bats also eat fruit.

Some bats snatch fish from the water with their feet.

Amazing facts

Giraffes are the tallest animals of all, at over 16 feet from head to toe.

An elephant eats more than 400 pounds of food, and drinks 53 gallons of water, every day.

A hippopotamus can hold its breath for about four minutes while it is under the water. Some seals can stay under water for about 45 minutes. And some whales dive for more than an hour before coming up for air.

The slowest mammal is the sloth, which spends its life hanging upside down in the trees of South American forests. It never moves faster than half a mile per hour. The fastest animal, the cheetah, is on page 30.

Birds

What is a bird?

All birds have feathers and wings, and most birds can fly.

pigeon

When a bird flaps its wings, the feathers push the air back and down, so the bird moves forward and up.

When winter comes, some birds fly thousands of miles to find warmer countries. This is called migration.

All birds lay eggs. A baby hatches out of the egg by cracking the shell.

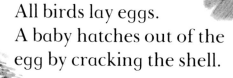

A bird's eyes are usually on either side of its head. So it can see almost everything around it. It hears well too.

Birds have no teeth. Instead, they have a hard beak or bill.

Birds have two feet, with claws for gripping.

 # Feathers

Birds are the only animals with feathers. Feathers give birds their colors and help to keep them warm.

starling

puffin

flamingo

hoopoe

golden
pheasant

swallow

hummingbird

parrots

ostrich

A tiny hummingbird
beats its wings 60
times a second.

The huge ostrich cannot fly,
but it can run very fast.

51

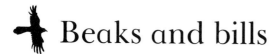

Beaks and bills

Bills and feet give clues as to what birds eat.

toucan

Toucans have long, strong bills for pushing leaves apart and picking fruit and nuts.

sparrow

wren

Sparrows have stubby little bills for crushing seeds. Wrens have pointed beaks for snatching insects.

curlew

Curlews have long, thin bills for poking into sand and mud.

golden
eagle

Eagles are called birds of prey.
Birds of prey have long, sharp talons for
holding their prey, and sharp, curved beaks
for tearing meat.

Pelicans scoop up
fish in their huge
beaks.

pelicans

53

Nests

Birds build nests for their eggs. The nests must be safe from their enemies – either out of reach or hidden away.

storks

The stork builds a big, untidy nest of twigs, high up.

The tailorbird makes a neat little nest. It sews two leaves together.

1

2

The woodpecker makes
a hole in a tree for
its nest.

The chaffinch uses soft
moss and feathers in its
cozy nest.

chaffinch   woodpecker

3

4

 # Eggs

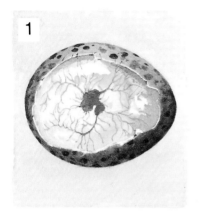

An egg contains food and water for the tiny embryo inside the shell. The embryo grows into a chick, which gets bigger and bigger.

chaffinch

hoopoe

golden eagle

56

herring gull

3

herring gull chick

Then the shell cracks and the chick crawls
out — this is called hatching. Different birds
lay eggs of different size and color.

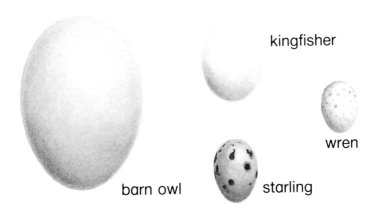

kingfisher

wren

barn owl   starling

57

 Night hunter

The barn owl lays its eggs in holes or on bare ledges, often in empty buildings.

When the eggs hatch, the owl finds food for its chicks. This owl has caught a rat.

Owls are nocturnal. They sleep during the day and hunt at night.

Soon the chicks will learn how to fly and hunt. Then they will leave the nest.

59

 # Swimmers and divers

Some birds spend a lot of their time on the water. Penguins dive through the sea to catch fish. They cannot fly, but they use their wings as flippers when they swim.

Birds clean and smooth their feathers with their beaks. This is called preening.

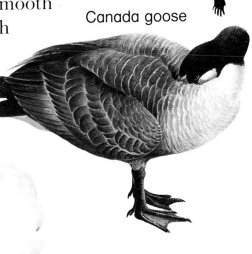

Canada goose

swans

Most water birds have short, powerful legs with webbed feet. They use their feet as paddles in the water.

mallard ducks

Some birds catch fish and other small animals in the water. Others feed on plants.

Kingfishers

The kingfisher perches by a stream. It has a red oil in its eyes which blocks the glare from the water and lets it see fish below.

When the kingfisher sees a fish, it dives into the water with folded wings. It grabs the fish with its strong, pointed beak.

The kingfisher uses its wings to swim up to the surface, and flies back to its perch. Then it tosses the fish into the air and swallows it whole, head first.

The kingfisher shakes off any water and preens its feathers, ready for another dive. Each dive lasts only a second.

Amazing facts

 Each year the Arctic tern flies across the world, from the Arctic to the Antarctic and back again. That's about 25,000 miles altogether.

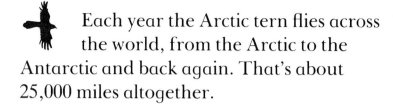 Storks have no voice — but they make loud clapping noises with their beaks.

 Ostriches are the biggest birds, and they lay the biggest eggs: each egg is about 6 inches long.

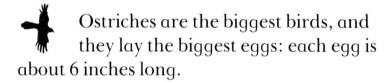 The spine-tailed swift is the fastest bird. It can fly at 90 miles per hour.

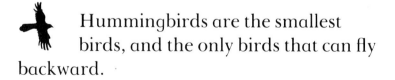 Hummingbirds are the smallest birds, and the only birds that can fly backward.

Reptiles

What is a reptile?

Crocodiles, snakes, lizards, tortoises, and turtles are all reptiles. Dinosaurs, which lived long ago, were reptiles too.

Reptiles have scaly skin. Many of them are brightly colored, like this lizard.

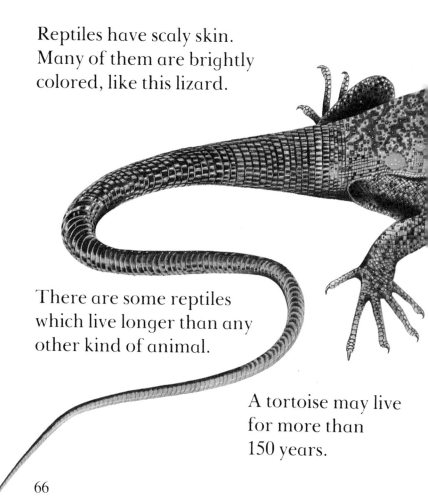

There are some reptiles which live longer than any other kind of animal.

A tortoise may live for more than 150 years.

Reptiles are cold-blooded animals. This means that they cannot keep their bodies warm in cold weather. They need lots of sunshine to keep warm. That is why most reptiles live in hot countries.

If they get too hot, they hurry into the shade or into some cool water.

ocellated lizard

Some reptiles give birth to live young, but most lay eggs. Their eggs are not hard like birds' eggs, but soft and leathery.

Reptiles that live in cold countries hibernate during the winter and wake up in the spring.

Chameleons

The chameleon is a lizard that lives in trees.
It grips the branches with its tail and toes.

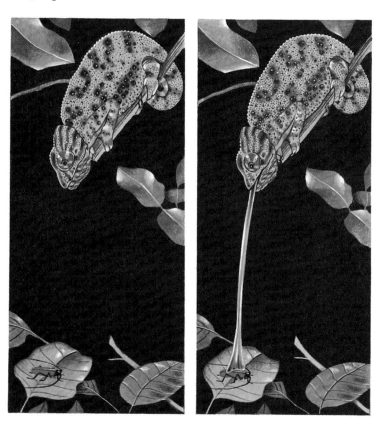

It catches insects by shooting out its sticky
tongue and pulling them into its mouth.

Chameleons are usually green or brown, but they can change color to match their background. This is called camouflage, and it helps them to hide from their enemies.

Chameleons also turn dark when they are angry, and pale when they are afraid.

🐢 New skins

Lizards and snakes grow a new skin when they get bigger and the old skin gets tight, or when the skin is scratched and worn.

They hide away and lie still for a few days. An oil spreads out between the old skin and the new skin. The old skin becomes dry and loose, and its colors grow dull. Now it is ready to be shed.

banded gecko

Lizards rub themselves against rocks and other rough surfaces and tear off the old skin little by little. The new skin is underneath.

This king snake is hatching from its egg. As it grows, it will shed its skin every month or two.

king snake

The snake rubs its head against something rough until the old skin splits open. Then the snake wriggles out. The skin comes off in one piece.

 # Snakes

All snakes are carnivores. They can open their mouths very wide to swallow animals that are bigger than they are. Snakes do not chew their food — they swallow it whole.

Some snakes use poison to kill their prey. When the snake bites, its fangs inject poison into the victim. Poisonous snakes often warn large animals to keep away by hissing or spitting or rattling their tails.

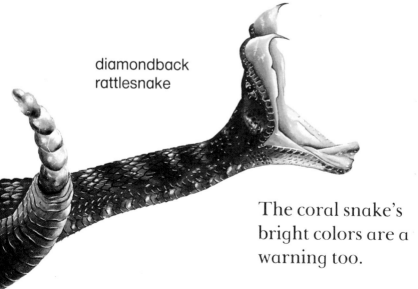

diamondback
rattlesnake

The coral snake's bright colors are a warning too.

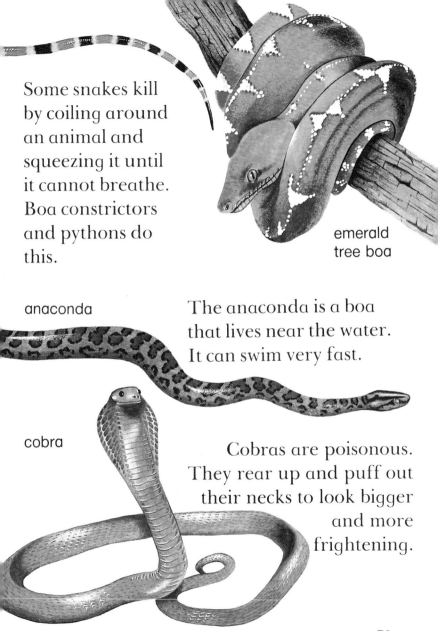

Some snakes kill by coiling around an animal and squeezing it until it cannot breathe. Boa constrictors and pythons do this.

emerald tree boa

anaconda

The anaconda is a boa that lives near the water. It can swim very fast.

cobra

Cobras are poisonous. They rear up and puff out their necks to look bigger and more frightening.

73

 # Crocodiles

Crocodiles and alligators are the biggest reptiles. Some are 18 feet long.

Crocodiles live in rivers, in hot countries, and they are powerful swimmers. With only their nostrils showing, they wait for animals that come to the river to drink. Then they seize their prey with their huge jaws.

Crocodiles look fierce, but they are good parents. They guard their nests of eggs and look after the babies when they hatch.

 Turtles

With their heavy shells, turtles move slowly on land. But they spend most of the time in the sea, and they are fast swimmers. They eat fish and other animals, and seaweed too.

Turtles lay their eggs on dry land. The green turtle digs a hole on the beach.

She lays lots of eggs in the nest and covers it with sand again. Then she goes back to sea. When the babies hatch, they make for the sea. Many are eaten by birds on the way.

Giant tortoises

Tortoises live on land. They are herbivores and feed on leaves, fruit, and grass. They have no teeth, but they have a mouth like a beak, with a hard bite.

The giant tortoise is about 30 inches high and 70 inches long. It weighs more than 400 pounds.

When a tortoise is frightened, it can pull its head and legs into its shell. Then it is safe from most of its enemies.

Amazing facts

Lizards can snap off their tails when they are attacked. The attacker is left with just the tail, and the lizard escapes. It can grow a new tail.

The largest lizard is the Komodo dragon. It is up to 10 feet long, and it often eats goats and small deer.

Crocodiles often lie on the river bank with their mouths open. This helps them to keep cool, just as a dog cools down by sticking its tongue out.

The alligator snapping turtle has a wormlike tip on its tongue. It sits in the water with its mouth open, and when a fish comes to investigate the "worm," the turtle snaps it up.

Amphibians

What is an amphibian?

Frogs, toads, newts, and salamanders are all amphibians. An amphibian begins its life as an egg laid in water. A tadpole hatches from the egg. When the tadpole turns into an adult, it leaves the water.

Amphibians cannot live in salt water, so there are none in the sea.

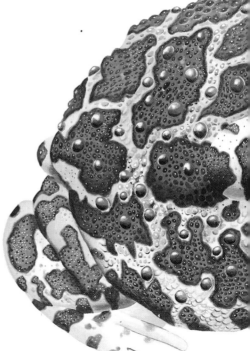

Frogs and toads have long, powerful back legs for jumping and swimming.

They use their webbed feet like paddles in the water.

Amphibians have two big eyes at the top of their head, so they can see all around.
They have a good sense of smell, too, even under water.

Frogs and toads catch spiders and other small animals with their long tongues.

European green toad

Like reptiles, amphibians are cold-blooded animals. But they have soft, moist skin without scales.

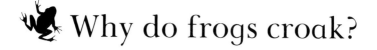 # Why do frogs croak?

Because amphibians are cold-blooded, they hide away and hibernate during the winter. They return to the water in the spring, when it is warm.

reed frog

In the spring, the male frogs and toads puff up their throats and make loud croaking noises to attract the females. After mating, the females lay their eggs in the water.

The eggs hatch into tadpoles. At first, the tadpoles breathe through gills, like fish. They eat plants in the water. They develop legs and lungs, and their tails disappear.

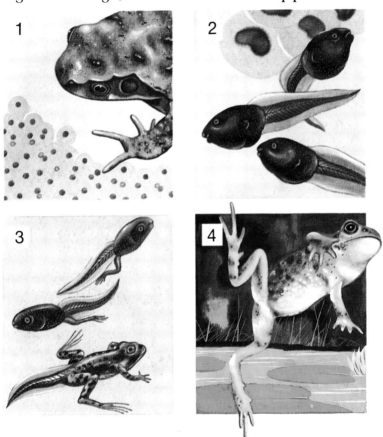

After four months, the young frogs leave the water to hunt small animals on land.

 # Tree frogs

Some frogs live in trees. Suction pads on their toes grip the twigs and leaves. Tree frogs are tiny, and often very colorful.

Newts and salamanders

Newts are amphibians that keep their tails all through their lives. Some of the newts that live on land are called salamanders.

great crested newt

fire salamander

Alpine salamander

smooth newt

long-tailed salamander

Amazing facts

The world's most poisonous animal is an amphibian – the poison arrow frog of Costa Rica in Central America.

The Goliath frog is the world's biggest frog. It is about 12 inches long.

Some frogs carry their eggs around with them, in their mouths or in pouches on their backs.

Spadefoot toads live in the desert and come out only in the rainy season. Their tadpoles have to grow up very quickly, before the water dries up again.

The giant salamander is the largest amphibian. It is nearly 7 feet long.

Fish

What is a fish?

A fish spends its whole life in water. Some fish live in the sea, some in rivers and lakes. Their bodies are usually covered with scales.

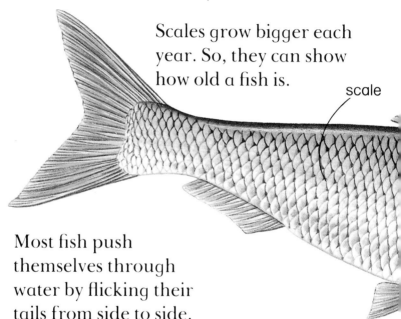

Scales grow bigger each year. So, they can show how old a fish is.

scale

Most fish push themselves through water by flicking their tails from side to side.

eggs

Fish steer themselves with their fins. They also use their fins as brakes, to slow down.

Like all animals, fish need oxygen to live.
We get our oxygen from the air we breathe,
but fish get theirs from water.

Water enters the fish's mouth and passes
over its gills, which absorb the oxygen.
Then the water goes out through gill slits
at the side of the head.

fin

Fish have no eyelids,
so their eyes are
always open.

gill slits

herring

Most fish lay eggs. This herring lays
thousands of eggs at a time. The eggs have
no shells, and many are eaten by other fish.
Only a few hatch into babies.

Scales, fins, and tails

Fish are all sorts of shapes and colors and sizes.

piranha

The **butterfly fish** has a big spot like an eye, to confuse its enemies.

The **porcupine fish** puffs itself up to look bigger.

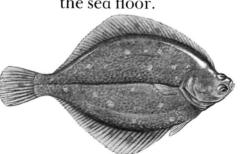

The flat, speckled **flounder** is hard to see on the sea floor.

The **seahorse** swims by using a fin on its back, not its tail.

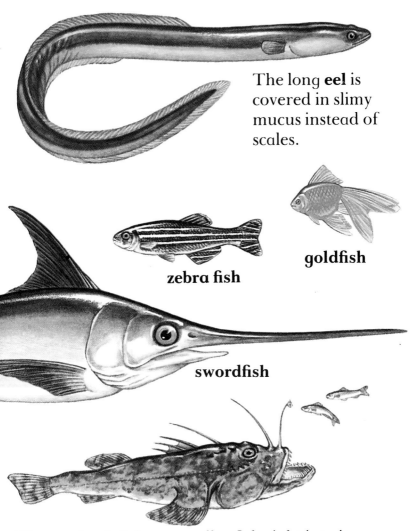

The long **eel** is covered in slimy mucus instead of scales.

goldfish

zebra fish

swordfish

The **angler fish** lures smaller fish right into its mouth by waving a long slender spine with a little flap of skin on it.

93

🐟 Sharks

Some fish feed on plants in the water, and some feed on other fish.

Sharks eat animals of any kind. They are fast swimmers and fierce hunters.

Sharks have a good sense of smell, which helps them find their prey. These two sharks are great white sharks. They are hunting a dolphin.

Great whites are known as "man-eaters" because they sometimes attack people.

A salmon's journey

Salmon have an amazing life. They hatch in rivers, and then they swim down to the sea. When they are ready to breed, they swim all the way back from the sea to the rivers where they were born.

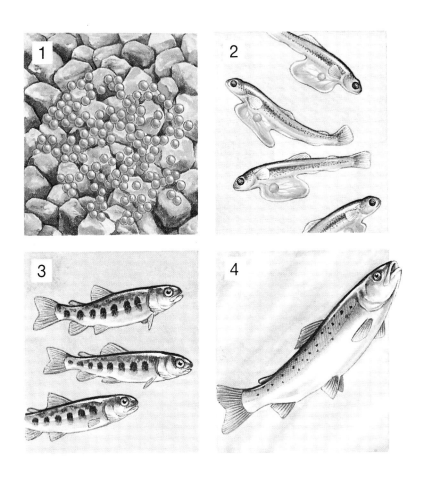

The female lays her eggs on the river bed.
When they hatch, the babies are called fry.
After six weeks they grow into parr. They
live in the river for two years and become
smolts. Then they swim down to the sea.

Amazing facts

The whale shark is the largest fish. It can weigh over 45 tons. Its skin is about 8 inches thick, the thickest of all animal skins.

The sailfish is the fastest fish. It can swim at 68 miles per hour.

The female seahorse lays her eggs in a pouch on the male's body. When the eggs hatch, the male pushes the babies out of the pouch.

The archer fish spits water at insects resting on leaves overhanging the river, and eats the insects when they fall.

Some Pacific salmon swim as much as 5,000 miles out to the ocean, and 5,000 miles back to the rivers where they lay their eggs.

Other

animals

🦋 Mollusks

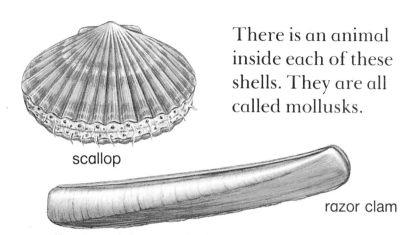

There is an animal inside each of these shells. They are all called mollusks.

scallop

razor clam

Mollusks with two shells live in water. They filter tiny bits of food from the water. When they sense danger, they close up their shells.

mussel

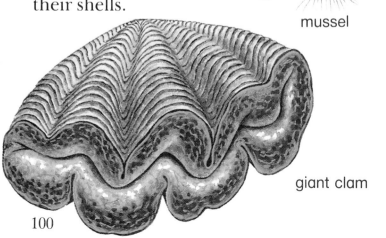

giant clam

100

top shell

On land and in water, there are some mollusks with just one shell.

They can pull their bodies back inside their shell to protect themselves.

nautilus

queen conch

Snails have no legs. They crawl along on one muscular foot.

sea snail

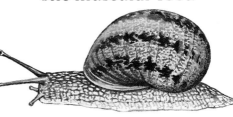
garden snail

101

🦋 More mollusks

Some mollusks have no shells, and many of these live in the sea. Others living on land are covered with slime to keep their bodies moist.

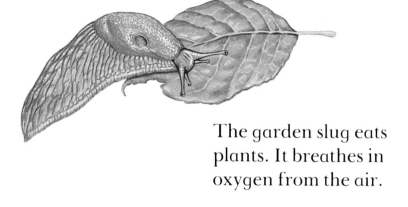

The garden slug eats plants. It breathes in oxygen from the air.

The sea slug absorbs its oxygen from water, through gills on its back. It feeds on tiny animals in the water.

The octopus is one of the biggest mollusks.
It has eight long arms and grips its prey
with the suckers underneath.

🦋 Crustaceans

The animals here are called crustaceans.
They all have a tough, crusty covering.
They have to molt, or shed, these
coverings as they grow bigger.

Long feelers help
crustaceans
to find
their way
around.

lobster

Lobsters and
crabs have
ten legs.

They use their huge claws for protecting
themselves and for picking up food.

shore crab

Crabs and lobsters scuttle over the sea bed. Some are also good swimmers.

The hermit crab lives inside an old shell. As it grows, it moves to bigger shells.

hermit crab

Shrimp have ten legs for walking, and more for swimming.

shrimp

barnacle

Barnacles open up their shells and wave their feathery legs to catch bits of food floating past.

🦋 Spiders

Spiders have eight legs. They belong to a group of animals called arachnids.

Spiders build webs with silk. They pull threads of silk from tiny spinnerets.

spinneret

house spider

eye

palp

This house spider builds big, messy sheets of silk. Insects get tangled up in the silk, and the spider eats them.

The spider's feet are covered in oil, so it does not get stuck in its own silk.

Many spiders can walk up walls and across ceilings because their feet have hairy pads for extra grip.

The biggest spiders are the bird-eating spiders. Some of them measure 10 inches across — big enough to cover a dinner plate.

Most spiders have two rows of four eyes — that's eight eyes altogether.

But spiders don't see very well. They have sensitive hairs on their legs and two feelers, called palps, to help them find their way around.

As they get bigger, spiders grow new skins and shed their old ones.

107

🦋 A spider's web

This is how the garden spider builds its web. First it spins a bridge thread. Then it adds spokes. It finishes with a spiral of sticky silk.

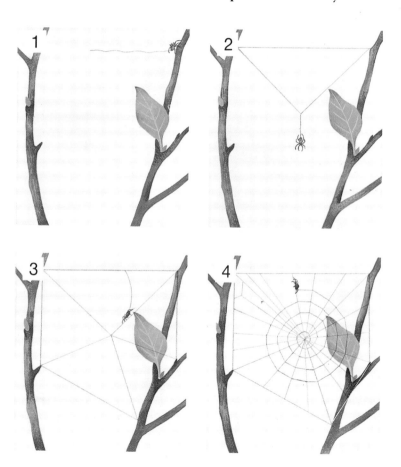

When a fly gets caught in the web, the
spider can feel vibrations along the threads.
It finds the fly and bites it with poison fangs.
Then it wraps the fly in silk and eats it.

🦋 What is an insect?

Insects have six legs, and most insects can fly. Some insects have one pair of wings; some have two pairs.

This ladybug has two pairs of wings. The front wings are hard, and they cover the delicate back wings when the ladybug is not flying.

The hard wings are brightly colored, to warn other animals that the ladybug tastes bad.

Every insect's body has three parts: a head at the front, a thorax in the middle, and an abdomen at the back.

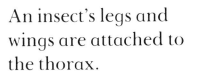

An insect's legs and wings are attached to the thorax.

Insects have two eyes and can see all around.

They also have two antennae to help them feel and smell things.

eye

antenna

Ladybugs feed on tiny insects called aphids.

aphid

Some insects have mouths that suck like straws. But ladybugs have jaws for biting.

🦋 More insects

There are about 1 million kinds of insects.
That means there are more insects than any
other kind of animal.

ants

cricket

stink bugs

ladybugs

large blue butterfly

bumblebee

housefly

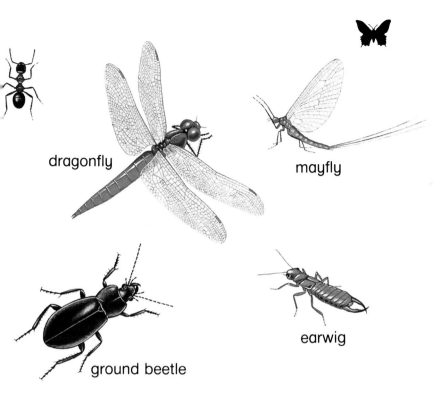

dragonfly

mayfly

ground beetle

earwig

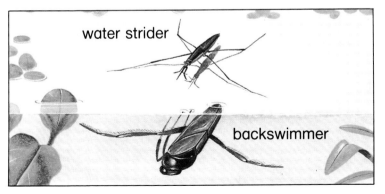

water strider

backswimmer

113

🦋 Butterflies

Insects lay eggs. This swallowtail butterfly lays eggs on a plant that her babies will be able to eat. She flies away before they hatch.

Out of each egg comes a caterpillar. It eats a lot and grows quickly.

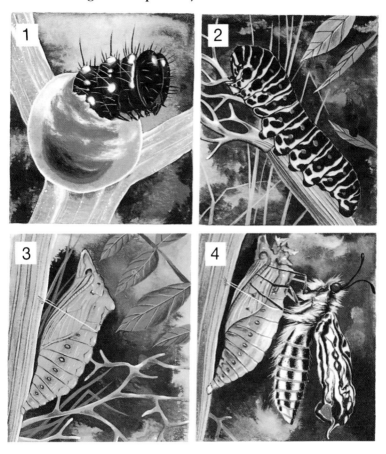

Then the caterpillar stops growing and turns into a chrysalis. The chrysalis splits open and a beautiful butterfly crawls out.

🦋 A wasps' nest

Some insects live in large groups. There may be 8,000 wasps in just one nest.

In spring, a queen wasp scrapes slivers of wood from trees, chews it up, and mixes it with her saliva. She uses this to build a nest with rooms called cells.

The queen lays one egg in each cell. When the eggs hatch into larvae, she catches insects to feed them. The larvae grow into adults and leave the cells.

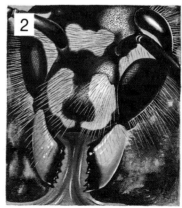

The new adults are the workers. They take over the nest building and find food for the queen and her next batch of larvae.

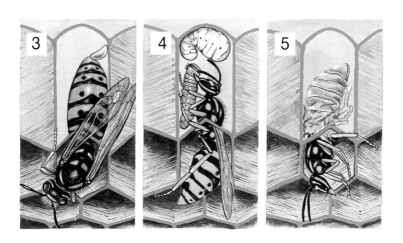

 # Worms

Earthworms belong to a group of animals called annelids. They have no eyes, ears, or legs.

Earthworms spend their lives under the ground, tunneling. Tiny bristles help them grip the soil as they wriggle along.

Earthworms swallow soil while they make their tunnels. They digest the dead plants that are in the soil and push the rest up above ground. These small heaps of leftovers are called worm casts.

worm cast

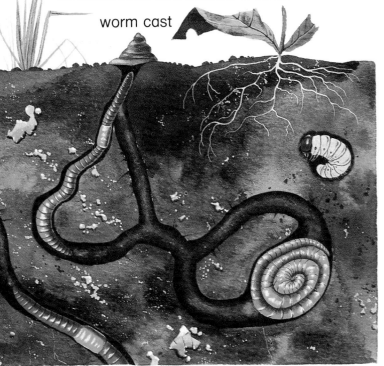

At night, earthworms come to the surface to look for dead leaves. They pull the leaves into their burrows to eat there in safety.

119

Amazing facts

The world's longest animal is an invertebrate – the bootlace worm. The biggest are nearly 200 feet long.

The spitting spider catches its prey by spitting sticky threads of gum over it so that it cannot move.

The biggest webs belong to the *Nephila* spider, in Southeast Asia. They are nearly 7 feet across. The silk is so strong that people use the webs as fishing nets.

The coconut crab lives on land and climbs trees to get fruit to eat, including coconuts that have broken open.

The earwig licks her eggs and babies to keep them clean.

INDEX